T0069214

THE MAN WHO LOST HIS HEAD

WINNER OF THE 2010 OMNIDAWN
CHAPBOOK CONTEST

THE MAN WHO LOST HIS HEAD

ZACH SAVICH

OMNIDAWN PUBLISHING

RICHMOND, CALIFORNIA

2011

Cover Art Courtesy of the Trustees of the National Library of Scotland
Cover and Interior Design by Cassandra Smith

Typefaces: Adobe Jenson Pro and Castellar MT Std

Printed in the United States
on archival, acid-free Glatfelter 60 lb. Natural Digital Smooth paper
by McNaughton & Gunn, Inc., Saline, Michigan

Library of Congress Cataloging-in-Publication Data

Savich, Zach.
The man who lost his head / Zach Savich.
p. cm.
ISBN 978-1-890650-50-6 (pbk. : alk. paper)
I. Title.
PS3619.A858M26 2011
811'.6—dc22
2010052019

Published by Omnidawn Publishing, Richmond, California
www.omnidawn.com   (510) 237-5472   (800) 792-4957
10 9 8 7 6 5 4 3 2 1
ISBN: 978-1-890650-50-6

For Jess Lacher and Tyler Meier

Pyrocumulous: the firestorm constructs its own weather, around

as the leaves resembled from a hollowed apple, the peel,

a railstorm, pondstorm, constructing, there cannot be

another beginning only insistence that this is of the first instance continuing (*To apple*

meaning to pick apples or to quarter something

as one would an apple or [appellation]

to name), a memoir of the higher frequencies, so the demand is less

expression of a soul than to locate where it is left,

fabric scrap on limb—is this it?—or it is a signaling of—*this way*—

These days of disinheritance / October
asks: you wanna salve / salvage / salvation /
I'm done with Dante / is it easier to make
a lion out of a rug or a sandwich / I used
to ask / I think the first leads to the last /
on the bus / a woman with a voice
so palpable, soothed / no one minds her on
the phone / she doesn't know if there will
be time for dinner before the film / river
brighter through the older bridge / you
can see it only from the new / where I grew
up everything was an hour's drive / west
was further east / I bought tomatoes at
the roadside stall / between breakdown and
impound, an easement / one's head here
does not clear / the river moves enough to turn
a body / held in place / by / it's far from me to say

Icicle slides down a power line,
a bead. All light noon-light,
to a degree: a few degrees of noon-

light low on the wind vane's
ankle charm. Sun never moves.
Hawks' lines of flight, iced.

Calmness of light in old houses, bricks
in Flemish bond, alternating header
and stretcher. Tulip poplars poking

around a miniature chapel.
These things are knowledgable, deep
sills in the thick walls and explanation

is only apology, no idea worth a grain
once it is memory. *Dear*. All
food being solely appetite

suppressant, I stir the oats. The paint
chips toward. Last night moonlight
dispersed out cloud, ringed like a roof

hole one might view it through.
Does *dark* mean *blank?* I drew a dark
each time one asked after you.

There's nothing in this light you cannot
see. Definitively: Cooper's hawk
in the apple tree. In the locust tree,

through the painted clays of sycamores.
I fell a hundred score. Brought home
a hundred shoveled tablecloths,

a single still-sizzling snowflake
wrapped in the classifieds. *Dear.*
Seed in snow falling or blowing,

of desire you said what made you
a wolf has now made you a woman.
Liked marketers for their ultimate

faith in longing. As you stood
in a doorway near a sea.
Lissome, in dissembling sheets.

Early light. Your room occuring to me
as snow does to a mountain.
All light a mobile's beads.

Magnolia offering blossom now
to the first hour's thaw
(there is no false thaw, even an hour's).

Can explain anything. How orphan
swans imprint to their handler's
hands—there's Leda for you, awash

with *orphic* swans. And here is
the snowling junco on seasoned
wood. *Snow-long.* One may be

many things, and have a temperature,
and all the emotions made for men
as sun was for the shed roof's tin.

Ice slides from a slant sloughing
tracks to the shingles, snow atop
stopped cars like siren bars.

Fields in cloud-caught light. Streets
salt white near sun-eroded brick.
The light's hanging perforations like

phone slips on a pole's poster
for something lost. There are no narratives,
economics, or theology, only the geologic

triad: heat, pressure, time.
Dear. Have seen the need to go
to extremes so they won't come

for you. Snow no longer melting
but melted to its presences, re-adhering
outside the frozen swamp by billboards blank

or hand-painted or billboards dark.
Rising fog. Hand-painted ice.
Insist: there is nothing that is not green.

I press the coffee grounds against my teeth /
and find you in your own life / watching
the lovers quicken their pace, leaving /
and who first tasted an alligator pear? /
eternity not diminishing urgency / like a man
at a party excitedly relating a story only
his wife now listens to / and has heard better /
and so what any poem could be called
Beginning or Joy or This Morning, Loved /
maybe we were wrong about it all / and all
was actually only effortless / and everything
that happens barely happens once / enough
to call me Shore Leave / Garden Part / call me
You Don't Need to Apologize But Once

But here is how it appears to one dying—but what if

we've been wrong about it all, and may act as every day's an armistice,

put out, like a dish of withering plums

with the sense many must have of breathing not only forever inward, granular,

gradually building only a vantage from which one

may witness where she has been. They say in every country she is

from the country, formerly a coast struck at angles to locate, eyes

as a runaway truck's ruts, smoothed to a sandy,

now lifting, now spritzing with rye. I am whatever is between hat,

glasses, and beard, hitting a note toward you from varied haggard positions—

whatever it is to "be known"—

To act forever comprehending how little this was

(an *I had a feeling*) (cursive of vein)

forever departing in the instance continuing for hills

or a dimness making hues we can manage

where one bends to the hummingbird-processed water

one then exists no more than. Numbness

literaler than pain, foregrounding feeling at the edges, strange

fidelities: two tomatoes on the table were a bulbous bird,

his story beginning: *Therefore by the end you will understand*

why my present style is so brazen—so bland—

Identity being merely manners,

second-hand grace while soldiers

line for review. *Aspiration*

is only breath. Sun coming around

like an obsolete horoscope,

sun coming through. *Dear*. Dared

read only by the phonograph.

What's not to love? Face,

easily imagined transfigured,

flagrant as a leg in a skirt in cold

weather. Smile to me like you do

to yourself, that apt gladness spreading

eye to eye: quick cut. Sky

the color of the ligamented space

among bones in an x-ray.

Saw-tooth clouds, a human error,

your full name in a registry,

like appliances. You should not know

what you are making, the emperor explained.

I forgot Andy is trying to assemble a full
deck from only cards he finds on the street or
a friend does / then today: the Four of Clubs,
which he already has / done with travel,
travels in love / done with waking oddly,
deep waking, bent waking, knee bone waking /
clouds move like a pulled plug or hospital
gown / I take it in like the formerly pregnant
girl tells her dressmaker to / boyfriend in
his car out back / his sweater the color of river
film / in this film they dub even the screams

Her dress we called The Entire
Snowy Firs Unhappening. Of Superman,
the docile language student's

tutor explained "he cannot hurt"
may mean he does not
cause pain or feel it. Leaden floods deflowered

us through small towns near Homestead
and Tulle. Saw the curled vine iced,
as though frozen in motion though

veritably grown steadily to that curling, still
who knows more than a word
or two for starlight on the concrete dam?

Troubled now by transformation,
you into this me into that,
while my desire is steadiness. Troubled

now by transformation, you into this
me into that, while my
desire exceeds imagining. *Dear.* A time

when description was enough.
Field thick as a bottle's ridged lip.
It has been years and you lived alone

on a small coast with little but the education
we have in common. (She had so many
names for colors and flowers, they blended.)

Dear. One finds in the imbalance, ballast.
Explaining only offers synonyms,
yet takes me back, in no condition,

hesitation where heartache was,
grasses soft as an idea we got behind.
It is no way to live, a centerfold

of chimney smoke reorganizing portage
clouds, but has its charm: the river
barge passes land where they use guitars for purses,

new sorts of glass, a periscopic hand.
What are we going for?
Dear. Let's make each other feel good,

at least this once. Life was a misunderstanding
of how life ends, the opera singer said
among the disentrenching palms. One filled

the draftiest crafts with batting the robins
tore to streams. In light of the glistening
whir of your embrochure bent to as to a drive-

through's box, in light of the eventual,
radiant—name one thing I wouldn't give and I
will summon it. *Dear*. Barrel

marked with beaded leaden script: *choice
evaporated winter apples*. What I thought
warned of thinking nothing

lasts warned of thinking nothing lasts
except in memory, I saw retrieving this volume
from the widow's drawer, from all her tiny

vials of tempered glass. *Dear*. You
were in touch, were in my arms
themselves, marked me with fevers

I panted for and quelled, an acolyte
of older cosmologies. I knew without a glance,
ate the cheapest roots, brewed chicory

and unencumbered rice, boilt spelt
grains by extract of fireworm withdrawn
from the first-time pregnant

woman's heel. Thus from the heat,
I carmelized, an older tale.
Stoa meaning colonnade, this philosophy

was named for strolling under it. Sun
on dark wood, so one grows apart. A *stoic*
is an ambler. *Dear*. Nothing

walks without stirring the bottom up.
The *post-script* precedes the peak of correspondence's
exchange. That is when I look up and think of you.

As looking up in the thesaurus, that is,
every sight referring back to you.
Noon. Rain laid in the lowest tread. Rose

garden in full sun, how do they not dry?
Snow now like a lady's neat hand-
writing across the hand-cut sky. Of course,

we know next to nothing of the concerto's actual
instrumentation or pace, let alone
volume or if a breeze on one's fingers during

a rest were accounted for.

I suppose I do believe in nothing / some were
literally skipping / football on screen a choreography
mimetic of egg smell and leaves / found fondness
deepening, and forgiving, as all failed more /
I suppose one could get interested in things / technology,
pragmatic jokes, purple sweatshirts, concession stands /
yet we do not have feelings but everything else
through them / as who could tell one feeling's cause
from what one in it latches to / the proprietor passed
her hard candy so she could not bite her nails /
I could not read Beckett because it seemed too much
like everything / I could not tell if I had read all of Beckett
or merely gone outside

I suppose I do believe in nothing / though there is
geometry, of ass and martini glass / my bus schedule
tattoo, responsive, postbox mouth / leaves underfoot gone
pulpy until they're merely water / and in my soul
a bowling lane's hard won clatter / man at the
laundromat stripped, his head in a machine / flowers in
the windowseat of an empty store

I suppose I do believe in nothing / legs

unmoving but the skirt they're still in does /

to be expert merely in the langors of light /

light notching the retrofitted façade

like lyrics on a karaoke monitor / less expensive

to diagnose by watching any film

I feel I am wearing a hat but am not. Can't even tell
if I'm sad or sick. Shared a yawn with a bus
stranger. All we've ever done is variously revise
Leaves of Grass. To leave then at the height of one's—
to leave off—sun stranded across the sky like a piano two men carry
uptown—

A Children's Story:

The village woke and every word was hell—

Hell hell hell hell hell

And every word they wrote was hell.
And numbers, too.
And the sound little birds made, animating the copper oxen bells.
And when you said your name, hell sashayed from you—

Dear. Rejected for the brain study,
I surveyed a portfolio of blossoms.
Went then near donkeys. They could

teach me little but bray. Come closer now
(meet me on the once-crossed plain).
Here is a little bit of innocence.

Try to forget. Try to absorb it. Come
closer now (meet me at the well-dressed river).
Chandelier in the balcony

known as The Lady of the House.
A tarnished tinsel firmament flares
off truck bumpers. Little metallic asterisks, in rain

close enough to see through. I see
the exquisite embers and wind the mind is.
Dear. Spitting blood into wine, the mind

is a little bit of innocence thrashed
on a once-crossed plain. Now give me something
new to miss, beyond the obvious.

Make it flash like trout in a pan.
Dear. Can't you get closer: lyricism results
from adoring precision more than detail.

Poems and coins first appeared in 350 BC
coinage currency tender.
Dear. The tree doesn't fall far.

You can't metabolize grace. Salt-fingered
ends of haystacks, trees in wind
like coats in the river. River like a coat

folded on an arm. Hold on to my arm.
You can't metabolize desire, thus, we confuse
it with grace. The scar arrives.

Sun a jerked out tablecloth.
Sun above us like a percolator's hole—

And yet

Only to be initial to another. I live a chip off the block from
Paradise Road. Paralyze?

Find the mortal world enough. But where have you been—
stayed out all night—like the milk you warned me about—

But then it's cold enough you don't mind the light.
Makes the blue look white. Makes me look

surprisingly easy—that's one kind of beautiful. Another is
I've counted the eggs.

I've counted

In bed like fishing flies in their case
choice evaporated winter apples printed on the antique scrap

And days all was riding on puns, days of disinheritance we welcomed
like an estate sale of blades, day dreary enough you could smile

at anyone

If Love exists why remember

It is not betrayal

if you stoop to a tooth

near curb

handkerchief it

and we never meet

I suppose I do believe in nothing / the live thing brown
in a bright bush: earthy swallows / and loneliness, a rain
washed out wanted poster / can't our solution be
it's not a problem? / pyrocumulous / the forest fire
conducts its own weathered system / electric razor smelling
of an old camera and the white floral room at the
rear of a dank church the priest goes brightly to / the tears
are wax / candles warmed by hand which preserves
the wick much as you might think the soul / at the library
she stamps each inside page and I feel similarly marked /
they cut everything they could from the eunuch thinking
it might make his song ever more pure

Zach Savich is the author of *Full Catastrophe Living*, winner of the 2008 Iowa Poetry Prize, and *Annulments*, winner of the 2010 Colorado Prize for Poetry. His most recent book, *The Firestorm*, is forthcoming from the Cleveland State University Poetry Center.

Zach Savich's *The Man Who Lost His Head*
wrestles with the irrational rationality of life as
we dimly perceive it. Yet these poems elicit, like
the ambiguity of life itself, our most fervent and
strange fidelities. There's such a thing as a willed
poetic ignorance: it forms its own epistemological
haven, and these poems live in that locale. Thus
the poet can ask "Does dark mean blank?" and, in
the very asking, expand the horizon of possibility
(that is, knowing) by which we recognize the
interchangeability of absence and desire. In that
dark, we grope into and through the rudiments
of our own longing, "melted to its presences."
When Savich writes "I suppose I do believe
in nothing," his words resound as a positive
statement of belief.

–Elizabeth Robinson

$11.95
ISBN 978-1-890650-50-6
51195>

9 781890 650506

OMNIDAWN®